MOOSE!
The Reading Dog

By Laura Bruneau and Beverly Timmons
Illustrated by Mic Ru

Purdue University Press, West Lafayette, Indiana

Library of Congress Cataloging-in-Publication Data

Names: Bruneau, Laura, 1976– author. | Ru, Mic, illustrator.
Title: Moose! the reading dog / written by Laura Bruneau and
    Beverly Timmons ; illustrated by Mic Ru.
Description: West Lafayette, Indiana : Purdue University Press,
    [2018] | Series: New directions in the human-animal bond |
    Audience: Age 7–9.
Identifiers: LCCN 2017060480 | ISBN 9781557538130 (pbk. : alk.
    paper)
Subjects: LCSH: Working dogs—Juvenile literature. | Dogs—
    Therapeutic use—Juvenile literature. | Human-animal
    relationships— Juvenile literature.
Classification: LCC SF428.2 .B78 2018 | DDC 636.73—dc23 LC
    record available at https://lccn.loc.gov/2017060480

Contents

Chapter 1
About Me

Hi! My name is Moose. Moose is a good name for me because I'm very big. I weigh over 100 pounds!

But don't worry, I'm very friendly. In fact, it's my job to be friendly.

I am a reading dog. Does that sound silly? Dogs don't read!

Reading dogs help children enjoy reading.

Let

me

tell you

my

story!

I'm a mixed Saint Bernard–Australian Cattle Dog. My mom and dad were both working dogs.

Working

dogs

like

to work.

Saint Bernard dogs are good at finding people who get lost in the snow. Cattle dogs are good at herding cows.

Because my mom and dad were working dogs, I was born to be a working dog, too.

I was born in Colorado, where
there are many huge
cattle ranches.

Cattle dogs
round up cows
so they don't
eat all the
grass.

Rounding up cows was what my
brothers, sisters, and I
were born to do.

I tried to herd the cows, but that was boring. The cows were so slow!

I liked to run after the horses. I would nip at their hooves. Now that was fun!

And so I'd forget about the cows.

I was not

a good

herding dog.

The rancher made a tough choice. He loved me, but he needed dogs that work hard every day.

The rancher took me to an animal shelter. An animal shelter cares for animals that need a new home.

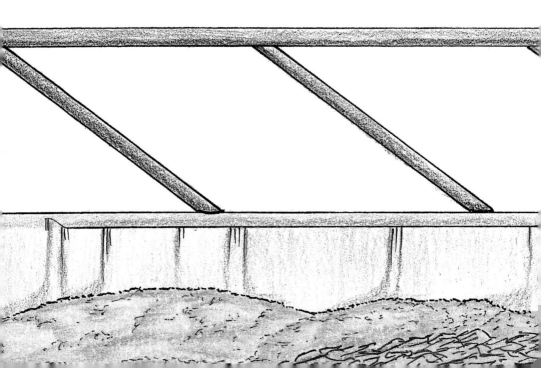

"You're a good, gentle dog, Moose," he said as he petted me goodbye.

"I know you'll find a good family who will play with you."

Chapter 2
The Shelter

I was sad to leave the ranch, but the animal shelter became my new home.

The people at the shelter were very kind. They fed me good food and played with me.

But sometimes they were too busy to play, and I was pretty lonely at night.

Rose, my favorite worker at the shelter, liked to say,

"Moose, you have the prettiest brown eyes and the cutest freckles."

I was the biggest dog at the shelter. I heard people talk about me. They called me the "gentle giant."

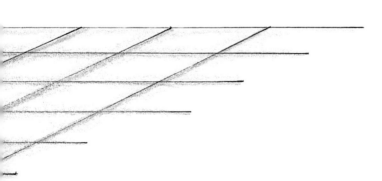

I made many dog friends at
the shelter. I loved to run
around with my friend
Maeby, a lovable
Pit Bull mix.

I also loved to
fetch sticks for
Winnie, a shy,
small dog.

Soon, Maeby was adopted by a dad and two boys, and Winnie went to live with an older woman.

I was happy my friends got a new home, but I felt sad that no one had chosen me.

"Just
you wait,
Moose,"
said Rose.
"We'll find
you a forever
home."

And guess what!

One morning a
young woman
walked in
the door. She
carried a photo
of me from the
newspaper.

The woman talked
to Rose. She said I
had a friendly face
and she wanted
to meet me!

We went for a walk. She tossed a ball, and I brought it back. I didn't get too excited—after all, I had played ball with people before.

I noticed the woman stayed longer and filled out forms. But then I watched her drive away!

I rested my head on my paws. Would anybody ever take me home?

The next morning Rose gently tied a red bandana around my neck. She seemed happy.

"You look very handsome today, Moose," she said.

"Hmm," I thought, "this is different."

Just then, a car pulled into the parking lot. Again, I didn't get too excited. Cars were always coming and going.

The woman came back! She was carrying a leash. She walked toward me with a big smile on her face.

"Hey, Moose," she called, "I'm Sally.
You're coming home
with me."

I wagged my tail and
jumped up and down.
I was so excited!

I bounded into the car.
I was going to my new home!

Chapter 3
My New Home

I loved my new home! It had

a big backyard to run around.

Inside, I had a soft, blue bed. I

even had my very own toys!

But the best thing about
my new home was Sally!

Sally played with me.
She fed me carrots and
yummy dog treats.

When I got sleepy, Sally
gently petted me
until I fell
sound
asleep.

I had to learn a few rules, though.

Cassidy, Sally's cat, did not like me very much. She was queen of the house. If I got too close to Cassidy, she would hiss.

And she had claws. "Ouch!"

I
learned
to let
her
sleep
in
peace.

When we went for walks, Sally put me on a leash. I had never walked with a leash before.

Such great smells!

Sally said, "Leave it."

Things to chase!

Sally said, "Heel, Moose."

"That's right," I thought.

"I must learn
the rules."

One morning,
Sally was in a hurry.

"I'm going to work today,"
Sally said.
"See you later, Moose."

I watched her leave.

"Why would Sally leave me?" I
wondered. "Will she come back?"

I missed Sally.

I chewed one of her shoes. The
shoes smelled liked Sally and
I felt better.

When Sally came home,

I was so happy to see her!

Sally was happy
to see me, too.
But then she
found her shoe.

"Oh, Moose,"
Sally said.
"Those were my
favorite shoes!

You need to learn
some rules."

Chapter 4
Learning the Rules

Sally and I went to obedience school.

I wanted to do things right!

I learned

sit,

down,

come, and

stay.

Sometimes it was hard, but we practiced and practiced. When Sally walked away, I wanted to follow her. But I had to sit very still and wait for her to say, **"Come, Moose."**

When I did things right, she petted me and gave me treats! She always said, **"Good dog, Moose."**

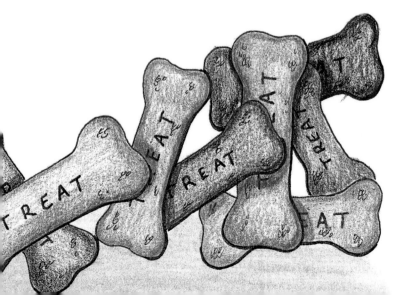

Even though I liked to play,
I learned quickly.

I was growing up and
following the rules.

My teacher said I was very smart.

"Moose seems to have a good sense about people," she told Sally.

Sally knew there was something special about me, too.

Because I liked people, Sally took
me to meet her friends.

Some of her friends had children.
The children petted me and we
would play fetch.

I loved being with the kids.

Sally noticed that although I was very
big, I was very gentle.

Sally took
me to see the
veterinarian. I was
growing fast and
needed a checkup
and shots.

"Moose, you are a pretty cool dog,"
said Dr. O'Malley.

He said that a lot.

Dr. O'Malley told Sally I had a patient and friendly temperament.

I was growing up and learning fast.

I came when Sally called my name.

I sat when she needed me to wait.

I did not chew Sally's shoes!

I was happy, but something was missing. Remember, I am a working dog. I want to be useful.

But what
kind of work
could I do?

Chapter 5

Getting Ready to Work

One day Sally said,

"Moose, I know what
you can do! You always
know when I'm feeling
sad and make me feel
better. You can be a
therapy dog!"

Sally knew about feelings because she
was a counselor. A counselor
helps children talk about
their feelings.

How do therapy dogs help children?

Sometimes it's hard for children to talk to adults. But things don't seem so scary when you have a friendly dog to pet!

Therapy dogs comfort children in hospitals, schools, and even in libraries.

Therapy dogs make people smile!

To become a therapy dog team, Sally and I went to special classes. We had new skills to learn!

A therapy dog must be calm when meeting new people. This skill was easy because I like making new friends!

But some skills were hard!

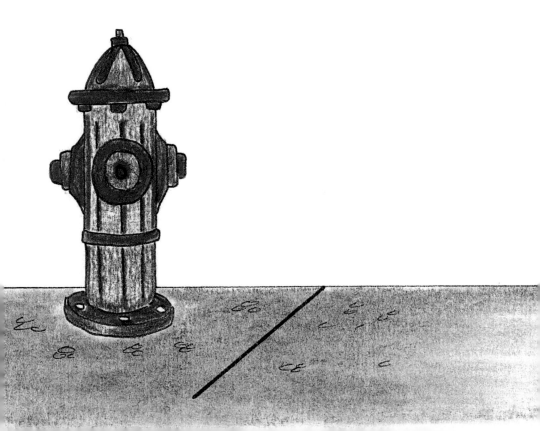

I learned to sit
quietly while
Sally talked
with someone
for a long time.

I learned to
walk through
crowds and
greet people.

Next, Sally and I had to pass a test.

On the big day, we took
a long car ride to the big
city. We walked into a tall
building. I even got to ride
in an elevator!

Sally and I quietly waited until my name
was called. I was so nervous!

But, we
passed the test!

They said I was a patient and
gentle therapy dog.

Soon after, Sally gave me my official
working uniform. It was an extra large
(of course!) green vest.

When a dog wears a vest, it tells people
he is working.

I was ready to work!

Chapter 6

I Am a Reading Dog

Sally and I got a very cool job! We are a reading dog team.

Every week, we visit schools and help children who are learning to read.

Learning to read is hard work!

Books have lots of long, new words.

Sometimes children are scared
to read out loud.

Sometimes children are
embarrassed when they make
a mistake.

And sometimes, children just
don't like to read!

New readers need to have a kind, patient listener. That's what Sally and I do—
we are patient listeners!

Before we visit, I get a bath. And I always wag my tail when I see Sally get out my special green vest.

When we get to school, I walk down a long hallway to my room. My picture is on the door.

The children call out,

"Look, it's Moose!"

Everyone is excited to see me!

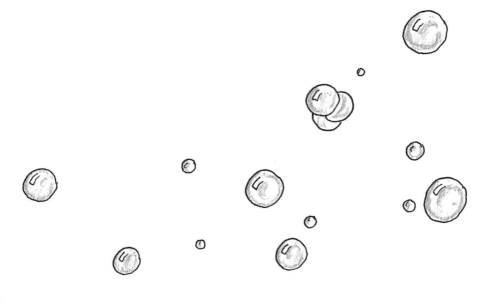

My room has comfy pillows and a rug. And lots of books! I really like books about animals.

When a child comes to read, I wag my tail to say, "Hello," and I sniff their hand.

Sally talks to the child for a bit.

I lie down to hear the child
read a book.

I sometimes close my eyes so I can **really** listen.

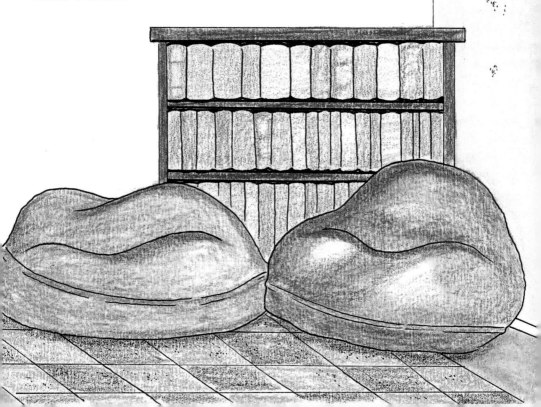

Sometimes children like to lie next to me.

Sometimes they show me the pictures.

Sometimes they tell me about the story.

But my favorite is when they hold my paw while reading.

Sally helps the children learn new words. And I help, too! Sally says I help children feel at ease.

And guess what!

When they are done reading, a child gives me a doggie treat. "Yum!"

The child hugs me goodbye. I am a little sad to say goodbye but happy to have helped.

Remember I told you I am a working dog?
Working dogs are happiest when we
are working!

I really like to be with people. My new job
lets me be with children and help them
practice their reading.

Being a reading dog is
just perfect for me!

Maybe I'll get to hear you read me a story someday!

How Reading Dogs Help Children

What Children Do:

1. Choose a "just right" book.

2. Say hello and pet the dog.

3. Sit in a comfy spot and read.

4. Show pictures to the dog.

5. Practice reading new words.

6. Talk about the story.

7. Say goodbye and give the dog a treat.

What Reading Dogs Do:

1. Get ready to visit with kids.

2. Wag tail and greet the child.

3. Lie down and get ready to listen.

4. Look at the pictures.

5. Give support to the reader.

6. Listen patiently.

7. Eat the treat!

About Moose!

Moose is a 115-pound male dog of mixed breed. He was adopted in 2009 by his owners, Laura Bruneau and Michael Wermes. A happy, free-spirited dog, Moose loves to hike in the mountains and chase squirrels in his backyard. He is a very calm, friendly dog. Everyone simply loves him. Through registration with Pet Partners, the largest therapy animal program in the country, Moose and Laura have been providing animal assisted interventions in their community since 2011. Previously, Moose and Laura were a Reading Education Assistance Dog (READ) team through Intermountain Therapy Animals.